Mikiala

O'AHU

LANIKAI BEACH

O'AHU

PALM TREE, NU'UANU PALI

LANIKAI BEACH WITH MOKULUA ISLANDS

O'AHU

Photography by **Douglas Peebles**

Text by **Jan TenBruggencate**

Mutual Publishing

Mutual Publishing

Library of Congress
Catalog Card Number 2001118533

Book Design
Michael Horton Design

Eighth Printing, April 2012

ISBN-10: 1-56647-508-2
ISBN-13: 978-1-56647-508-2

Mutual Publishing, LLC
1215 Center Street, Suite 210
Honolulu, Hawai'i 96816
Telephone (808) 732-1709
Fax (808) 734-4094
Email: info@mutualpublishing.com
www.mutualpublishing.com

Printed in China

TABLE OF CONTENTS

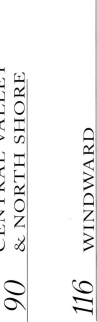

MOONRISE OVER
THE MOKULUAS

Photographer's note
PHOTOGRAPHER'S NOTE

AS A TRAVEL PHOTOGRAPHER, living in Hawai'i, I am often asked which is my favorite island. I usually come

up with some politically correct answer such as "I love them all equally, but each for its own different and special reasons."

The secret truth is I like O'ahu best and that is why I live here.

Waimanalo to Waianae, Kahuku to Hawai'i Kai, O'ahu has several communities that are unique, not only to Hawai'i but to all of Polynesia. Of course Waikiki is incomparable. I had lived on O'ahu for 20 years before I spent a night in Waikīkī. When I finally went to stay a few days with my family we discovered what we had been missing (Many other people already knew this). Surfing, outrigger canoeing, shopping, dining, Waikīkī is a fun place. It can be either as relaxing or exciting as you want to make it. The same can be said for the rest of O'ahu.

This book is a collection of my favorite photos of the island. Living here makes it possible to shoot with the best weather, so you can't expect it to look like this everyday. On O'ahu though, you should always be able to find something beautiful or interesting.

Douglas Peebles

WAIKĪKĪ

THE ISLAND OF O'AHU IS

HULA,
KĀNE'OHE BAY

Foreword FOREWORD

the beating economic heart of the Islands. It has two long mountain ranges, with a wide plain slung between them, and stunning green cliffs to

the north side and gently sloping sunny shores to the south. As the population and business center, it is of paramount importance in the Islands today, but Western society values things differently than did earlier residents. O'ahu was probably not the first of the Hawaiian Islands to be inhabited. Chances are, the initial voyagers sailing up from the Polynesian islands to the south first saw the massive volcanic peaks of the Big Island. If they left the Marquesas or Tahiti in the South Pacific summer, it would have been winter in the north, and those peaks might have been snowy-topped domes initially rising above the clouds on the horizon. Later, they would have picked out the top of Maui's great peak and, eventually, on a clear day, the islands beyond.

Eventually, O'ahu was populated by families in island-hopping canoes, and it didn't take long. The island sports some of the earliest dated archaeological sites in the chain.

But even then, to the Polynesians, O'ahu did not have the kind of singular importance among the Islands that it does today. Huge Hawai'i, the cluster of islands around Maui, and the isolated sisters of Kaua'i and Ni'ihau all had important benefits. O'ahu's finest feature—the potential of its deep and protected harbors—would not be recognized until more than a thousand years after the first habitation, when European ships

LEI STAND AT AIRPORT

DUKE KAHANAMOKU STATUE

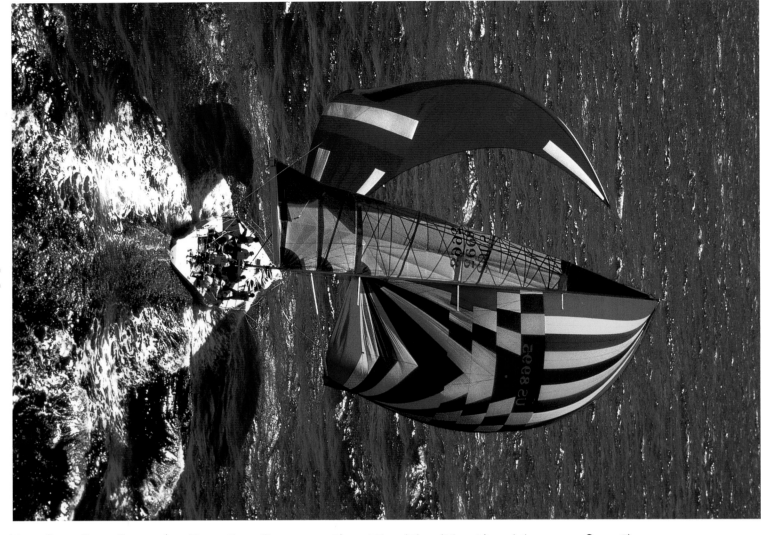

that had need of sheltered waters arrived. Hawaiian canoes, after all, could be hauled up on almost any shore to be made safe on land.

The royalty of the Islands in the days immediately after European contact kept their headquarters at their traditional favorite coastal sites—places like the Big Island's Kona coast and Maui's Lahaina. But soon enough, O'ahu and its broad south-facing bay, Honolulu, took on the mantle of capital. They never let go.

With increasing populations, the island's environment was changed. Humans reconfig-ured the island's nearly 600 square miles as needed. The wetland agricultural fields and duck ponds back of Waikīkī suited their time but, when new land was needed for hous-es and businesses, the wetlands were drained into the Ala Wai, a canal dug behind Waikīkī that led to the sea. When plantation agri-culture sought land for sugar and pineapple, wells pierced the island's aquifers, and tunnels were drilled from the wet windward

ORNAMENTAL BANANA, WINDWARD O'AHU

TUNA FISHING OFF WAI'ANAE

side to irrigate the great central O'ahu plain. When more harbor space than Honolulu Harbor could offer was needed, the reef fronting the 'Ewa pearl lagoons was blasted to create a deepwater entrance, forming Pearl Harbor. When housing demand grew, the vast marshes known as Kuapā Pond were dredged and reformed to create waterfront housing called Hawai'i Kai. O'ahu is arguably more changed than any of the other islands, but its vibrant mix of modern urban with tropical paradise is perhaps unique in the Pacific.

And there remain places that recall the early days of Hawai'i. Find them on the rugged eastern end of the island at Queen's Beach and Makapu'u and on the nature reserve at Ka'ena, on the western point. Find them on the narrow road north from Kāne'ohe on the windward side, on the reefs off the southern coast, deep in Moanalua Valley, on trails high in the Ko'olau and Wai'anae Mountains. And find them in the attitudes of Hawai'i's people, in the culture of the Islands.

Many sources translate the name of the island to mean "gathering place." It seems appropriate for the most populous of the Islands, but the most respected source on the subject says it's probably not correct. More likely, the name of the island is among those words "so ancient that no translation at all is possible," write the authors of *Place Names of Hawai'i*.

PALM TREE
AT SUNSET

LEIS, DOWNTOWN

HIBISCUS, WAIMEA FALLS PARK

PALM TREES, KAHANA BAY

A LOW COASTLINE OF

Chapter One
EAST O'AHU

protected waters sweeps eastward from Diamond Head, forming the wide, shallow Maunalua Bay. The bay is punctuated at both ends by volcanic features

FISHING, HĀLONA POINT

Diamond Head or Lē'ahi at the western end, and Koko Head at the east. They are the most prominent features visible from an aircraft approaching from the east, from a cruise ship slipping down the Kaiwi Channel on its run from San Francisco Harbor, or from an outrigger canoe making its way from Lā'au Point, on Moloka'i.

The area between the craters is one of O'ahu's primary residential areas, running from the costly homes of Kahala to the waterfront properties of Hawai'i Kai. Small, quiet beach parks mark the area, which is dominated by the residential nature of the region. The waters of the bay are somewhat protected by jutting Koko Head. It is a shallow reef coastline, which made it appropriate for conversion into fishponds by early Hawaiian residents. Unmortared stone walls were built out from the shore on the reef flats, enclosing several acres before curving back in to the coast. Today, many of these ponds have been filled and converted to high-priced beachfront housing.

At Hawai'i Kai, developer Henry Kaiser converted the old marshlands known as Kuapā Pond into lagoons lined

HANAUMA BAY

houses. The lagoon entrances are bridged to allow traffic to cross through the Portlock area into the rugged eastern mountains and beaches of the island, the area known as Kaiwi.

The highway rises up the slope of Koko Head. A one-mile trail leaves the highway and rises to the 642-foot summit of Koko Head, Kuamoʻo Kāne, which provides a wide view across the ocean to the south and the leeward side of the Koʻolau Mountains to the north. The waters off this point mark the western edge of the famed Molokaʻi Channel, one of the roughest bodies of water in the world. Athletes from around the world test themselves here in the classic outrigger canoe race, the Molokaʻi Hoe (*hoe* is the Hawaiian word for paddle), which starts at Hale O Lono on Molokaʻi's west side and crosses the channel to finish at Waikīkī. The race pits international crews in six-seat canoes against each other and against the Kaiwi Channel. Each fall, a men's race and a women's race draws hundreds of paddlers from Hawaiʻi, the Mainland, Canada, Australia, Tahiti, New Zealand, and European countries. More recent channel crossing events cater to paddleboards, kayaks and one- and two-seat outrigger canoes.

Koko Head in the afternoon sun shades the deep bay, Hanauma. Here, a marine reserve protects the fish resources, and divers can swim among the coral heads and find tame fish in all the colors of the rainbow. Hanauma is among the most stunning natural features of O'ahu, and visitors will see a variety and abundance of marine life seldom found in other parts of the island. Because it is so popular, the City and County of Honolulu has established some restrictions on the use of Hanauma, designed to preserve the bay despite its substantial visitor and resident traffic.

A short-drive distance down the rough, rocky coastline, waves wash into a cave in the cliff face. The force of the water drives air and foam and a column of water through a hole in the cave roof. When the surf is running, white geysers erupt with each swell, creating the attraction known as the Hālona Blowhole. There are similar features on several other islands as well. The next best known is Kaua'i's Spouting Horn, which, like Hālona, is on a rock shelf facing south.

Off to the right of the blowhole as you face the water, there is a tiny sand beach at the base of a steep trail. Moviegoers will recognize Hālona Beach as one made famous in the movie, *From Here to Eternity*, where Deborah Kerr and Burt Lancaster rolled in the shoreline waves. But here, and at the other beaches east of Hanauma Bay, any kind of

SANDY BEACH

running surf creates dangerous coastal conditions. Waves sneak up on the unaware, and even accomplished swimmers can be caught in rip currents that can quickly drag them away from shore.

The Koko Crater Botanical Garden is situated inside a volcanic cone, previously known as Kohelepelepe, that rises to 1,208 feet above sea level. The garden features a range of dryland plants. A rifle range and stables are nearby. As the coastal highway reaches the flatlands once more, the body-surfing meccas of Sandy Beach, and around the lighthouse at Makapu'u Point, Makapu'u Beach, mark the boundaries of a rough scrubland area that is important to O'ahu residents as one of the few entirely undeveloped parts of their island. Campers, anglers, divers and those simply seeking to be apart from the urban life of the Islands seek out the small coves and beaches here.

Makapu'u Point reaches 647 feet above sea level at the top of sheer cliffs that plunge into the Kaiwi Channel. Beyond, the island coastline turns to the northwest, and the shallow reef waters are punctuated with islets that provide predator-free sanctuaries for nesting seabirds.

KOKO HEAD MOONRISE

CRASHING WAVES, HĀLONA POINT

WINDSURFING, DIAMOND HEAD

MAKAPU‘U LIGHTHOUSE

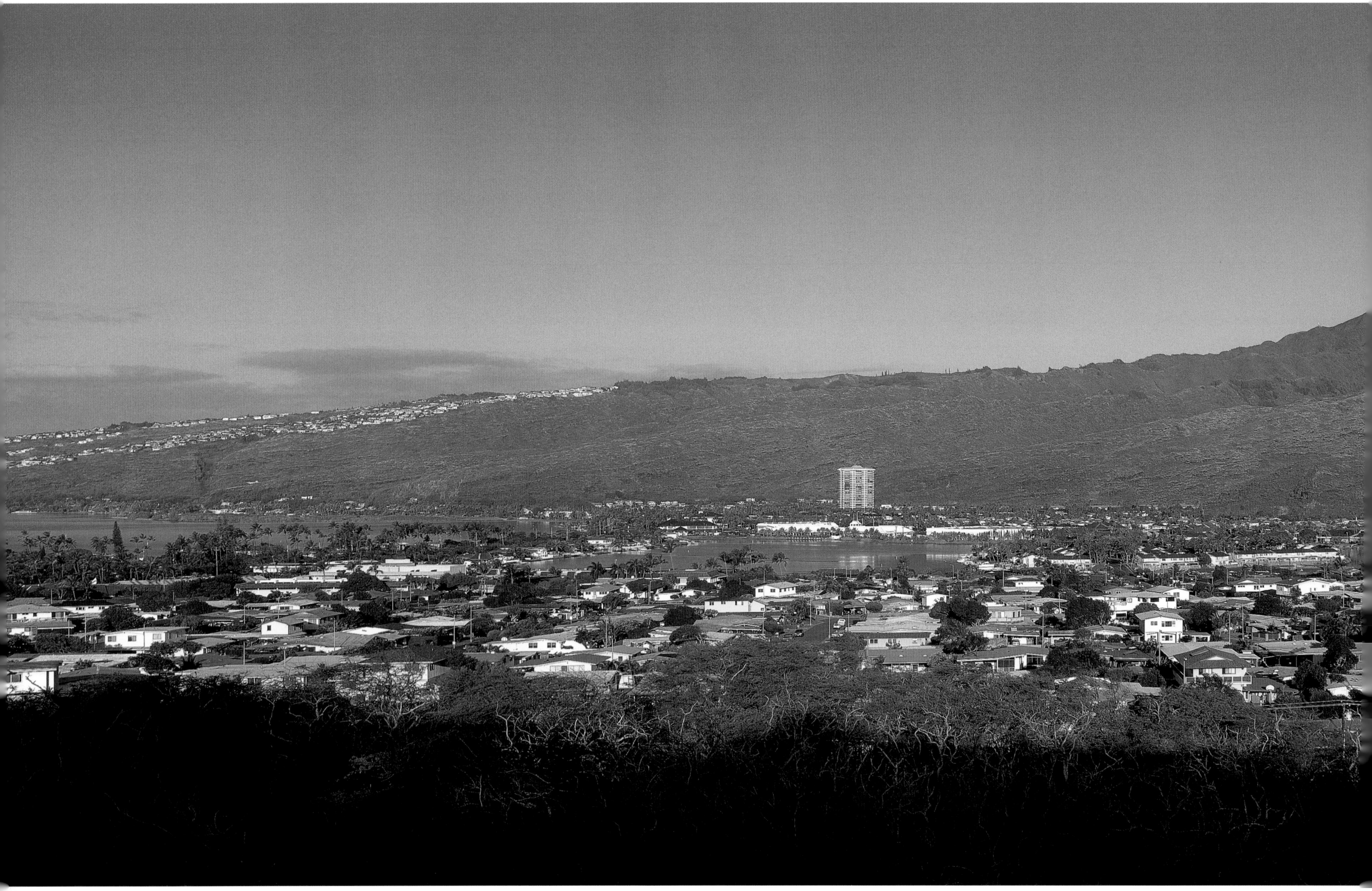

HAWAI'I KAI

MAKAPUʻU WITH RABBIT ISLAND

HĀLONA BAY *"FROM HERE TO ETERNITY BEACH"*

20

MAUNALUA BAY FROM KOKO HEAD
Following pages

DIAMOND HEAD LIGHTHOUSE AT SUNRISE

GREEN SEA TURTLE

OUTRIGGER SAILING CANOE,
MAUNALUA BAY AT SUNSET

DIAMOND HEAD LIGHTHOUSE AT SUNSET

'ĀINA HAINA AT SUNSET

BEYOND THE URBAN

ern side of Oʻahu that feels, perhaps, a little more like Hawaiʻi. Take a wander up the steep slope to the 761-foot summit of Lēʻahi, or Diamond Head, and find a vista that includes green unblemished mountains, a vast stretch of sea, the mottled greens, pale blues and browns of the reefs and, even in the urban areas, a sense that there is more vegetation in this city than most. The quiet neighborhoods are lined with trees of species that bespeak Hawaiʻi's present and its past, from the shiny leaves of the Polynesian kamani to the compound ones of spreading monkeypods from the tropical Americas. There are the artistically twisted branches of the flowering poinciana and the pan-tropical coconut palms.

The waters off Waikīkī have been a playland since the early days of human habitation here. Kings and queens of the islands surfed in the nearshore waters and kept homes along the calm waters. Inland, in those days before the canal called Ala Wai, or waterway, was built, the region directly back of the beach was rich with springs and water-filled fields of taro, with bananas and other crops growing on the dry land between the ponds. The region's name, Waikīkī, means spouting water and refers to these springs, which are now mostly gone.

Some of the finest music of Hawaiʻi has been composed and performed along these white sands. For old time residents,

Chapter Two
WAIKĪKĪ

experience of Waikīkī's lights, the tall hotels, the shopping and the night sights along Kalākaua and Kūhiō Avenues, there is a great deal of the south-

SAILING OFF DIAMOND HEAD

35

a walk along the strand recalls the sweet sounds of steel guitars and strumming 'ukulele, of voices quilted into fine harmonies, of beach-boy romances and surfing lessons, outrigger canoes and coconut trees.

The old Moana Hotel, a landmark on the beach for a hundred years, stands just down from the "Pink Palace," the Royal Hawaiian Hotel, built 26 years later. For the first half of the last century, these twin resorts were the tallest structures in the region.

Today, they are dwarfed by high-rises, but many residents still return regularly to the old hotels for a taste of a Hawai'i and a Waikīkī of times long past.

The western end of the beach is backed by Fort DeRussy, a military reservation that recalls Hawai'i's strong military connections. Members of the armed forces have vacationed here for decades.

You can walk the roughly two miles of Waikīkī Beach and find distinct cultures and feelings. There are regions where tanned surfers abound, and others where visitors in pale and burning skins inhabit beach towels. Just inland, the people-watching is as good,

VIEW FROM ATOP DIAMOND HEAD

TOUR CATAMARAN OFF WAIKĪKĪ

with visitors of all the cultures of the world wandering or marching purposefully, street performers and sidewalk exhibits, all surrounded by concrete and glass and an amazing amount of greenery for such an urban setting.

When the warrior king, Kamehameha, sailed from Molokaʻi to conquer Oʻahu, the reports say his canoes covered the shores from Waiʻalae to Waikīkī. He camped his armies at Waikīkī and prepared them for the coming battle against the forces of Kalanikupule. Although outnumbered, Kamehameha's forces which included an army of chiefly women who fought as musketeers broke through Kalanikupule's ranks and drove them up Nuʻuanu Valley. Later, Kamehameha would keep a home at Waikīkī.

At the eastern end of Waikīkī is one of Oʻahu's treasures, Kapiʻolani Park. This vast field holds ballparks and the Waikīkī Aquarium, a bandstand and a driving range, shade trees for family picnics, and the refurbished war memorial Natatorium, water features and tennis courts, and a multitude of places for contemplation.

At the western end of the beach, the Ala Wai Small Boat Harbor, where hundreds of fine yachts and not a few junkers live, marks the mouth of the canal of the same name. Beyond lies Ala Moana, the road by the sea. On the mauka or mountain side of the road, the Ala Moana Shopping Center attracts shoppers. Makai, or toward the sea, is the wide Ala Moana Beach Park, running from the man-made peninsula known as Magic Island to the Kewalo Basin, a small harbor where commercial fishing and tour boats dock. The beach at Ala Moana is one of the safest on the island. It is protected by a wide reef, and families with children regularly come here to swim, sunbathe and to picnic under the trees.

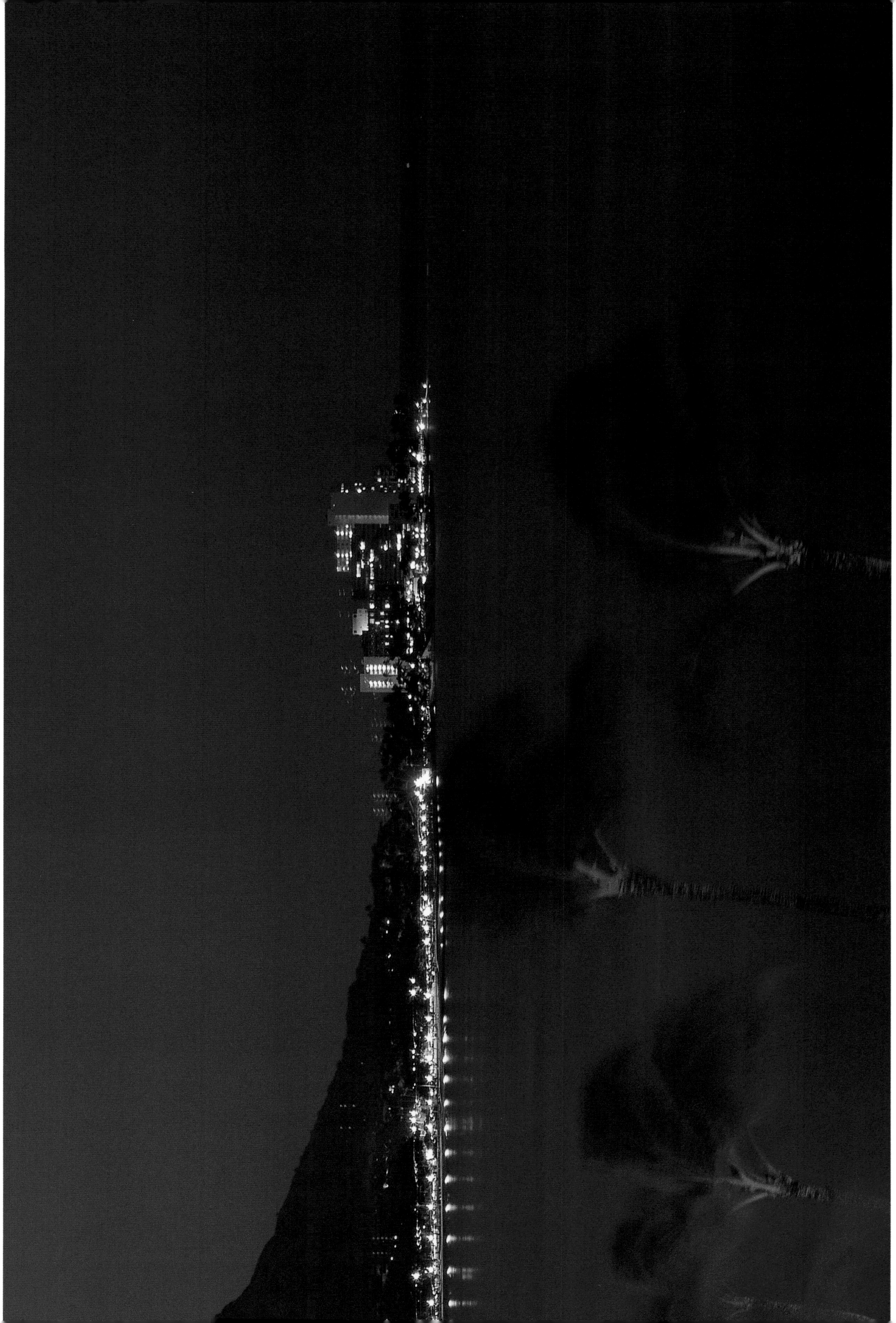

ROYAL HAWAIIAN HOTEL

TANDEM SURFING AT WAIKĪKĪ

HIKERS ON TOP OF DIAMOND HEAD

KIDS BODYBOARDING AT "THE WALL"

FRIDAY NIGHT SAILING RACES
Following pages

THE GLOW OF SUNSET ON WAIKĪKĪ

THE HEART OF

BROMELIAD
LYON ARBORETUM,
MĀNOA

Chapter Three
HONOLULU

urban Oʻahu is the region dominated on its coast by Honolulu International Airport and by the harbors of Honolulu, Keʻehi Lagoon, and the old lagoons now known as Pearl Harbor. Inland, it includes the valleys from Mānoa to and beyond the historic Nuʻuanu, with the highlands of Tantalus between.

Here was a zone that to early Hawaiians must have been a kind of paradise. The coastal waters were rich and mostly protected from the rough surf driven by the trade winds. There was a generally sunny leeward climate, but the mountains immediately back of the coast fed a series of rivers and streams, and a multitude of springs burbled up from the volcanic and limestone ground. It was a place of plentiful water, good climate and calm seas.

After Kamehameha's armies drove through this region routing the forces of the Oʻahu chief, Kalanikupule, he sought to ease the ravages of war by restoring the island's agricultural fruitfulness. Stories say he personally climbed the hill at ʻUalakaʻa to plant sweet potatoes, and that he ordered the taro fields replanted on the flats at Kapālama and Niuhelewai. The uniter of the Islands, Kamehameha had his enemies, but most of his people adored him, in part for his personal involvement. Even foreign visitors remarked on his activities. A skilled martial artist, he fought at the front lines in battle rather than directing events from the safety of the rear, as other chiefs might. In peace, he personally worked in the taro patches, doing the heavy work of cultivation, planting and harvesting. Early

MISSION HOUSES

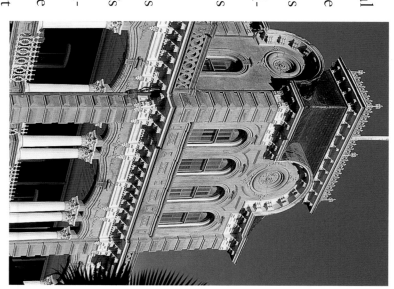

ʻIOLANI PALACE

European visitors expressed surprise in their journals that a king would do physical labor. He respected his people's religious traditions, and confined himself in the temple during the appropriate times.

Today, the agricultural nature of Honolulu region has been lost to commercial and residential pursuits. Mānoa Valley was one of the early sites for Westerners to live. Its fertility was recognized early, as well, and fields of pineapple and vegetables thrived here. Today, its deeper areas are old residential districts, and its lower reaches form the campus of the University of Hawai'i at Mānoa, the main campus of the statewide university system. Mānoa's east wall is Wa'ahila Ridge, which has a trail that leads from the residential community of St. Louis Heights to Awaawaloa, which some folks call Mount Olympus.

The west wall of Mānoa is dominated by Pu'u'ōhi'a, or Tantalus, which has a rural highland residential community and a fine network of forest trails.

Below Tantalus to the west is the neighborhood of Makiki, which rises on its western side onto the slopes of Pūowaina, or

SURFER, MAGIC ISLAND AT SUNSET

Punchbowl Crater, home of the National Memorial Cemetery of the Pacific. Immediately mauka of the crater lies the Hawaiian Home Lands settlement of Papakōlea, whose name refers to the Pacific golden plover, which walked the

FRIDAY NIGHT SAILING RACES, WAIKIKI YACHT CLUB

flatlands here during its annual winter visits to the Islands. The wide valley of Nuʻuanu, deep and green, which was favored for upland mountain homes to take advantage of the feature that translates its name: cool upland. Nuʻuanu was for much of Hawaiʻi's history the most direct route between Honolulu and the windward side. The old Pali Highway ran up the valley and then switchbacked down a mountain road to Kailua.

Today, the highway runs through a long tunnel to avoid the highest part of the mountain pass.

Downtown Honolulu was built as an adjunct to Honolulu Harbor. The early cart paths allowed merchants to go a short distance inland from their supply ships to their stores. Today, the heirs of those mercantile agencies, factors and banks still have their offices within walking distance of the harbor, but many are now multi-story concrete structures with reflective glass windows. And it is hardly a homogenous area. There are distinct differences between the varied

MĀNOA FALLS

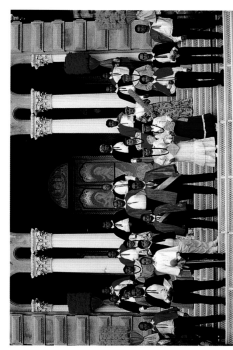

ethnicities of modern Chinatown, the sparkling financial district and the historic region. Several buildings that date deep into the 1800s, including the royal 'Iolani Palace, the royal office building, Ali'iolani Hale, which now houses the state's courts, and the oldest of the three, Kawaiaha'o Church, built of coral blocks chopped out of Honolulu's reefs.

Ke'ehi Lagoon, lying between Honolulu Harbor and Honolulu International Airport, has more of a link to the airport than many modern folks know. A flight over it on the way to or from O'ahu reveals the dredged seaplane runways, dating to a time when flying boats were the primary form of air transport between Hawai'i and the rest of the world.

Pearl Harbor, one of the primary reasons for U.S. interest in the Islands, is one of the largest sheltering places for ships in the Pacific. The entrance to the three-lobed lagoon was dredged to allow large vessels to enter. The events of December 7, 1941, when Japanese aircraft bombed the American ships there, have led to its development into both a high-security Naval base and a tourist destination. Visitors are attracted by the stark, white memorial to the sunken USS *Arizona*, the World War II submarine USS *Bowfin*, and by the restored 58,000-ton battleship USS *Missouri*. There are few pearl oysters left, due to environmental changes caused by both the runoff from the agricultural and urban areas uphill from Pearl Harbor, and the import of alien species growing on the hulls and living in the bilge water of ships.

ALOHA TOWER WITH USS *PATRIOT*

RAINBOW AND WATERFALL NUʻUANU VALLEY

AERIAL VIEW OF THE USS *ARIZONA* MEMORIAL

ALOHA TOWER

KING KAMEHAMEHA STATUE,
ADORNED WITH FLOWER LEIS

'IOLANI PALACE

AERIAL VIEW OF HONOLULU HARBOR

AERIAL VIEW OF DIAMOND HEAD
AND KAPIʻOLANI PARK

DOWNTOWN HONOLULU FROM PUNCHBOWL

KOʻOLAU MOUNTAINS FROM WAIMĀNALO,
WITH HONOLULU IN BACKGROUND

ABOVE THE USS *MISSOURI* IN PEARL HARBOR
WITH THE USS *ARIZONA* MEMORIAL IN BACKGROUND

SAILORS AND ANGLERS

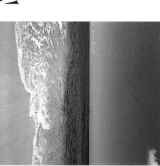

Chapter Four
LEEWARD

boating off the coast of O'ahu find a vast area of calm offshore, roughly from Barbers Point to Ka'ena Point. It is the lee formed by the massive

Wai'anae Range, a 20-mile-long spine of rugged green mountains that starts out heading northward just inland of Barbers Point and curves to the northwest as it approaches the westernmost point of the island at Ka'ena. Early each morning, a fleet of small fishing boats heads out of the harbor at Pōka'ī Bay to troll or bottom-fish in this gentle sea. Beyond the region, waters unprotected by the mountains are much rougher, and often specked with whitecaps driven by the trade winds.

The mountains cause the wind to slip up the eastern side of the range, dumping its moisture as rainfall on the windward slopes and summits. The leeward side of the range is a series of dry, sunny valleys. Modern-day Hawaiian culture thrives in this region, where canoe paddling, surfing, hula, and the Hawaiian sovereignty movement are active.

Going north, the communities of Nānākuli, Mā'ili, Wai'anae and Mākaha sit along a stunning coastline of white-sand beaches and black rock, with quiet streets that drift back into the dry valleys. Each community is fronted by a beach park, and several other coastal parks mark the region, although not all are good for swimming. Mākaha Beach Park features some of the best surfing. Visitors should be wary of the

water at any time when large waves are present, since most of the coast is not staffed with lifeguards.

Since the abandonment of the old dirt road and railroad that once connected this region with O'ahu's North Shore, Leeward O'ahu has been a driving dead-end, which most round-the-island tours miss. Efforts to develop resorts in this region have not done well, and Leeward O'ahu remains a strongly "local" bedroom community. It also has a strong military presence, which is the subject of some controversy among residents. The Navy controls most of vast Lualualei Valley and the Army uses Mākua Valley as a training and firing range. Environmental organizations are particularly critical of the Army's activities in Mākua because of wildfires caused by the live firing in past years, which have burned up into the native forest on the upper slopes of the valley. Fires have threatened several species of endangered plants and the beautiful striped O'ahu tree snails, of which every known species is endangered.

The state has designated the rugged eastern point of the island a natural area reserve, meaning it is protected for the range of native plants, insects, birds and other creatures found there. No vehicular traffic is allowed, but hiking is permitted,

AERIAL VIEW OF KA'ENA POINT, WITH 20-FOOT SURF

LANIKOHONUA BEACH

SUNSET, LANIKOHONUA BEACH

WAI'ANAE RANGE FROM OCEAN
OFF KA'ENA POINT

and coastal anglers favor the rocky coastline as they seek game fish like the ulua, more familiar to some as jack or pompano.

Ka'ena is said to be named for a male relative of the volcano goddess, Pele. The name is translated, appropriately enough, given this story, to mean "the heat." It can be dry and hot, but is often windy, as well, and swept by the salty winds off the sea. Many of the native plants here have been able to fend off invasive alien species because they are salt-tolerant coastal species, and are able to handle the inhospitable conditions better than non-natives.

The area is known in Hawaiian tradition as a leina, or jumping-off place, where the spirits of the dead would leap into the next world. Sometimes such a place has the more complete name, Leina a ka 'uhane, which translates to "leaping place of the spirits." Each of the Hawaiian islands has such a place, and some have several.

In Hawaiian tradition, stones can have power, sometimes have personality and often have stories. Off Ka'ena Point, there is a stone called Pōhaku o Kaua'i, or stone of Kaua'i. It is believed to be a stone originating on the island of Kaua'i, which is 60 miles across the Ka'ie'ie waho channel from here. One tradition suggests that a famous Kaua'i giant named Hā'upu threw the rock here.

MĀKUA VALLEY AND THE WAIʻANAE MOUNTAINS

MĀKAHA BEACH

KO OLINA

KO OLINA PALMS
Following pages

PAPAONEONE BEACH

KO OLINA AT SUNSET

KEAWA'ULA BEACH, ALSO KNOWN AS YOKOHAMA BEACH

THE TWO GREAT

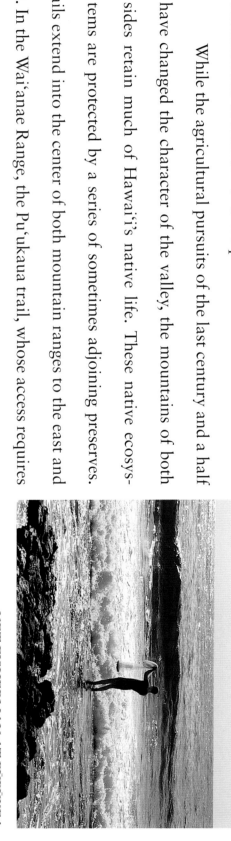

PIPELINE BODYBOARDER

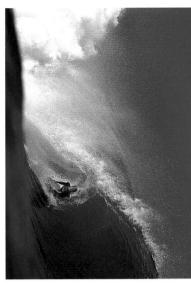

PINEAPPLE
DOLE PAVILION

Chapter Five
CENTRAL VALLEY
& NORTH SHORE

O'ahu, once dominated by broad fields of sugar and pineapple. While some pineapple fields survive, sugar is long gone from O'ahu, and many of the old fields have been replaced by housing and other urban and suburban developments. Much of the land is also occupied by the military, with Wheeler Air Force Base and Schofield Barracks being the largest of them.

The old plantation town of Waipahu and the southern end of the central valley, just above Pearl Harbor, and Wahiawā, dead center in the valley, recall the agricultural origins of the region. The newer communities of Mililani and Waipi'o lie between them.

While the agricultural pursuits of the last century and a half have changed the character of the valley, the mountains of both sides retain much of Hawai'i's native life. These native ecosystems are protected by a series of sometimes adjoining preserves.

Several hiking trails extend into the center of both mountain ranges to the east and west of Wahiawā. In the Wai'anae Range, the Pu'ukaua trail, whose access requires permission from The Nature Conservancy of Hawai'i, rises to the island's third highest peak, and takes hikers through prized native forest. Other trails require the permission of the Conservancy or the Army at Schofield Barracks. Folks can view one of the best bits of scenery on the island by driving through the Schofield gate and asking the way to Kolekole Pass, which allows an expansive view of both sides of the Wai'anae Range. Army per-

mountain chains of O'ahu, the Ko'olau and the Wai'anae, run in a southeast to northwest direction. Slung between them is the vast valley called Central

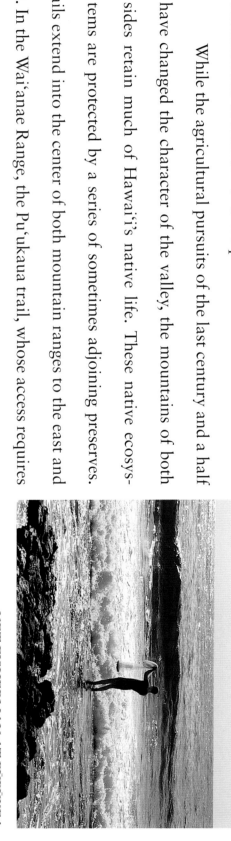

NET FISHERMAN AT PŪPŪKEA

mission is also required for the several trails on the slopes of the Ko'olau Range, across the valley.

At the northern end of the central valley, the terrain drops to a shore dominated in winter by surf generated in the storms of the North Pacific. O'ahu's North Shore is famous in surfing. Visitors who don't themselves surf come just to see the fantastic performances. At places like the Banzai Pipeline, the big waves break close enough to shore that the techniques of the aquatic athletes are visible without binoculars. At such times, swimming is hazardous, but during much of the year, when the water is calm, the wide, white-sand beaches of this coast, running from Kahuku Point down to Waialua Bay and on to Ka'ena Point, is a wonderland for beachgoers.

The commercial center for the North Shore is the bustling village of Hale'iwa, an old sugar town that now caters largely to visitors, but also to O'ahu's unique North Shore community of transients, professional surfers, professionals who can't abide living in the city, and a healthy contingent of what in the 1970s would have been called "flower people." This coastline has many features off the water and out of town. Waimea Falls, and the adventure park associated with it, attract many active folks, and the arboretum at the site is one of the state's premier botanic gardens. The stream from the falls flows down to Waimea Bay, a beautiful white-sand curve that is a county beach park.

The famed Puʻuomahuka heiau sits on a bluff overlooking the bay. This former temple of human sacrifice is one of the largest in the Islands, and has been designated a National Historical Landmark.

The western end of the North Shore, between Haleʻiwa and Kaʻena Point, is often quieter for being a dead end, and lacking the famed surfing spots of the other side. Here, the beach community of Mokulēʻia, and Mokulēʻia Beach Park lead to the flats where Dillingham Airfield, Oʻahu's second airport, is situated. This region is a favorite for gliders, which can operate from the somnolent field without much interference, and which can be seen cruising on the updrafts of the northern Waiʻanae Mountains. Just past the glider field, the 3.5 mile (each way) Keālia Trail leads hikers up a switchback trail ascending the cliffs, and then gradually upslope to the Kuaokalā Trail, eventually reaching an overlook to Mākua Valley, which falls way into Leeward Oʻahu. Farrington Highway ends a mile and a half past the runway, where a gate blocks access to the protected coastal terrain of the Kaʻena Point Natural Area Reserve.

WAIMEA SHORE BREAK

TIKI AND SURF SHOP, HALEʻIWA

DILLINGHAM AIRFIELD, MOKULĒʻIA

SUNSET BEACH

MOKULĒʻIA BEACH

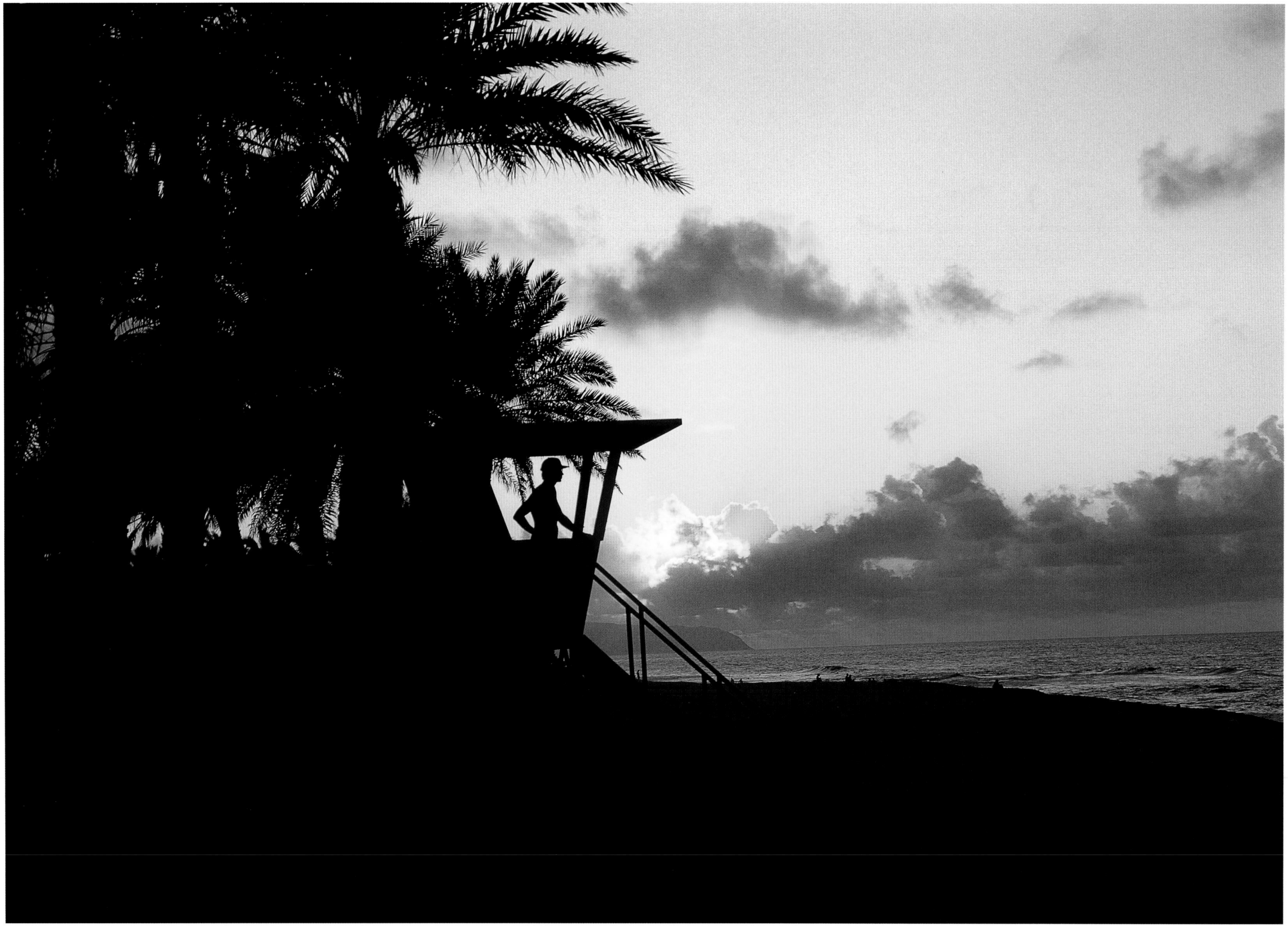

SUNSET BEACH LIFEGUARD STATION

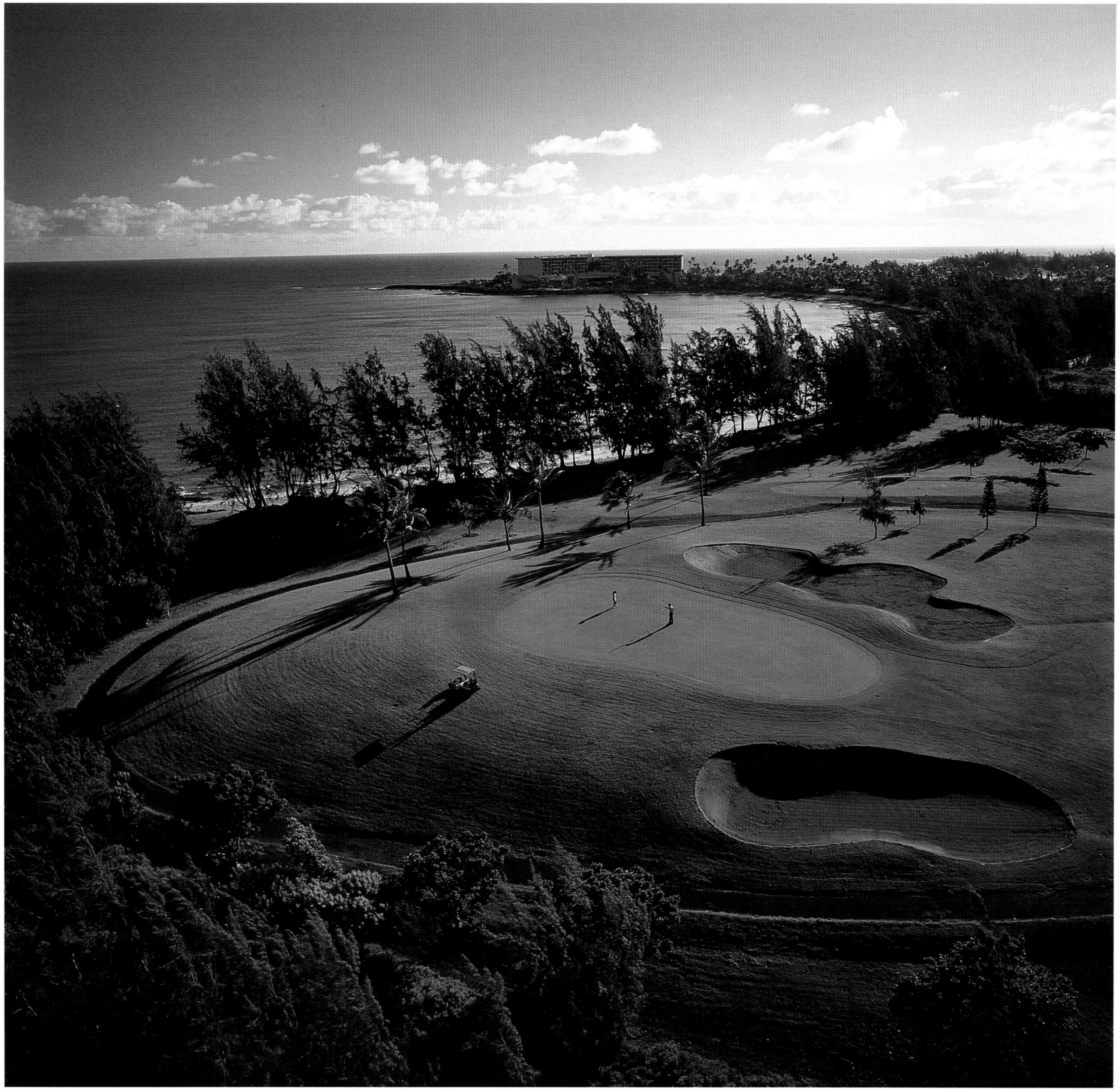

KUILIMA GOLF COURSE

SUNSET OVER KAWELA BAY

LARGE WAVES, PŪPŪKEA BEACH PARK
Following pages

AERIAL VIEW OF MOKULĒʻIA BEACH

MATSUMOTO SHAVE ICE, HALE'IWA

SUNSET FROM WAIMEA BAY 109
Following pages

BODYBOARDER, WAIMEA BAY

SURFERS IN THE EDDIE AIKAU CONTEST, WAIMEA BAY

Chapter Six

WINDWARD

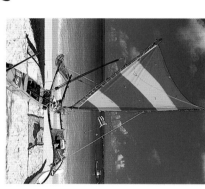

though only a few minutes away by car, is as far from Honolulu as you can imagine. Instead of a city full of high-rises, it is soaring green cliffs, verdant

THE WINDWARD SIDE,

**PETROGLYPHS,
WINDWARD OAHU**

valleys and a narrow strip of coastal land that leads to white-sand beaches and reefs with pale blue channels, yellow corals and algae that range from brown and green to purple and red. In its way, the Windward Side is more South Pacific than Hawai'i. It is a little bit of Ofu in the Samoan Manu'a Islands, of Bora Bora in the Societies. But with traffic.

The single road that runs along most of the Windward Side is a busy one, but many of the cars are rentals, and many stop only rarely, leaving the person who finds a special spot on a patch of sand oddly isolated, given the bustle that is often just a few yards away.

In some ways, the Windward Side is old O'ahu. There is a feeling of the history of Hawai'i that is as strong here as anywhere in the Islands. From the coastal community of Waimānalo to the southeast, to Kahuku to the northeast, this whole coastline faces the Pacific trade winds and, as a result, is normally breezier and cooler than the leeward sides of the island.

Geologically, this part of the island was once a sloping volcanic landscape that extended far beyond the present-day coastline. But in a titanic slide, one whole side of the island collapsed into the sea. The broken rocky debris of this prehistoric cataclysm is scattered out on the ocean floor for dozens of miles beyond the coast, visible through modern seafloor mapping equipment.

The great slide left a precipitous coastline that eroded into the sharp ridges and vertical gullies that stand at the back of Kāne'ohe. Their height helps create the weather of the area, as the trade winds rush up the cliffs, form clouds and dump rain.

O'ahu's two great Windward bays, Kāne'ohe and Kailua, have communities that are broad suburbs where many homes

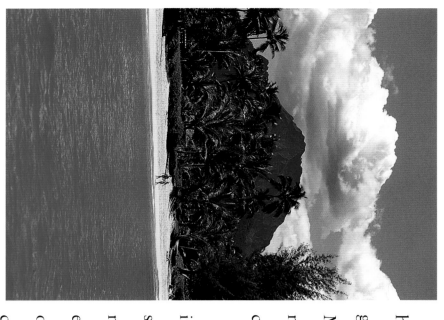

KAILUA BEACH PARK

MOUNT OLOMANA

have surfboards and windsurfing gear, fishing poles and canoe paddling equipment stashed in the garage. Overlooking Kailua is Olomana, rising to 1,640 feet between the valley community of Maunawili and the rest of Kailua. There is a rugged six-mile trail to the summit of Olomana, which hiking guides call one of the most dangerous hikes in the Islands.

The wide Kailua bay once came considerably farther inland, but siltation from the shore and blockages by sand bars filled it in, creating the Kawainui Marsh, a nature preserve frequented by wildlife and wildlife enthusiasts. The present-day bay is a wonderland for ocean recreation, from the most casual beach walking to the most aggressive kite surfing. Outrigger canoes sail and are paddled through these waters as they have been for centuries; only now, instead of the rich browns and golden colors of natural materials, they are flashy in all the colors of mod-ern sailcloth and carbon-fiber boat construction. Offshore islands just south of the Kailua beach community of Lanikai are favorite spots for picnicking residents.

Kailua Bay and the Lanikai coast are flanked by military installations, including the old Bellows Air Force Station to the south and the Marine Corps, air station at Kāneʻohe on the Mōkapu peninsula to the north.

Across the Oneawa Hills from Kailua, Kāneʻoheʻs flatlands, once prime farmland, are now largely residential subdivi-

sions and shopping complexes, fronted by a picturesque bay and backed by the incredible green cliffs. The bay contains some of the state's finest reefs and a collection of sand bars, low coral islands, and the memorably shaped Mokoliʻi Island, giving it the nickname "Chinaman's Hat." One of the treasures at the base of the mountains is the city's Hoʻomaluhia Botanical Garden, with hiking trails, assemblages of tropical plants and broad views of the entire Kāneʻohe region. On the coastal side of the Kāneʻohe subdivisions, Heʻeia State Park, tucked between a community pier and an ancient fishpond, provides fine views of the sea and mountains.

Northward along the windward coast, the trappings of suburbia quickly fall away as the cliffs move closer to the shore. Coastal parks provide access to the shore, which is generally well protected from the surf by the reefs. Except in periods of extreme surf or near deepwater channels, the shallow waters immediately fronting the sand and inland from the reef on the Windward Side are some of the safest for casual beachgoing.

Many of the residents of this region are long-time Hawaiʻi families. Many of the other homes, particularly those on the water, are weekend or vacation homes for residents whose primary abodes are in the city. The

CHINAMAN'S HAT, KĀNE'OHE BAY

AERIAL VIEW OF COCONUT ISLAND, KĀNE'OHE BAY

road twists and turns near the coast, sometimes right on the water, sometimes one beachfront lot back from the sea.

Looking to the mountains, viewers see cliffs that fall right to near the shore, but sometimes stand well back, forming high-walled valleys. The state has established parks in two of the major valleys of this region, both of which have hiking trails that carry walkers in between the valley walls at Kahana and Kaluanui. The latter valley has a scenic waterfall, known as Kaliuwa'a or Sacred Falls. (The park is known by the Western name, Sacred Falls State Park.) The trail to Sacred Falls has been closed in recent years after a rockfall in 1999 caused several deaths among hikers at the base of the gorge near the waterfall. Geologists warn that the near-vertical cliffs of Hawai'i can be unstable. In some areas, either excessively dry weather or heavy rain can prompt rockslides.

Near the northern end of the coast, at Lā'ie, the Mormon community has provided work for students at its Brigham Young University-Hawai'i by developing one of the finest Polynesian cultural experiences to be found in the Pacific the Polynesian Cultural Center. Here, students from around the Pacific provide visitors with views of cultures that otherwise would take thousands of flying miles to visit.

Northward lies the old sugar town of Kahuku, whose old sugar mill is now a small shopping complex, and, beyond that, the James Campbell National Wildlife Refuge is home to one of the finest displays of Hawaiian waterbirds.

WHALE BREACHING OFF KĀNEʻOHE

WAIĀHOLE BEACH PARK

MOKULUA ISLANDS SHOT FROM RIDGE ABOVE LANIKAI

MOKULUA ISLAND WITH HOBIE CAT

AERIAL VIEW OF WAIMĀNALO BEACH

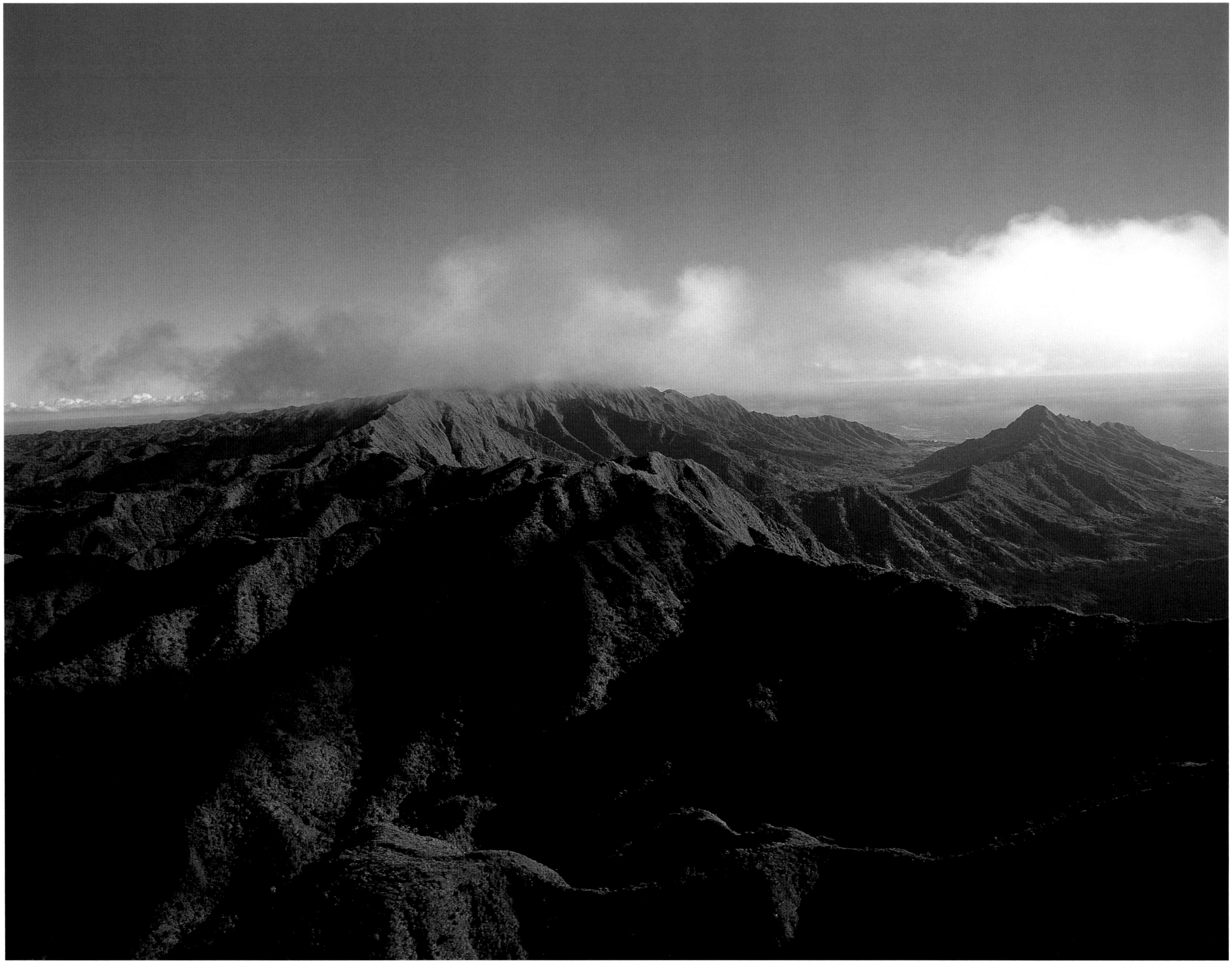

BIRD'S EYE VIEW OF THE KO'OLAU MOUNTAINS

O'AHU—SITE DESCRIPTIONS

Page i Lanikai was once named the best beach in the world. Although there have been problems with sand eroding from coastal properties, the beach and its nearshore waters remain an amazing place.

Page iii Royal palms, their trunks laden with heavy vine-like monstera plants, stand out against the sunlit walls and waterfalls of Nu'uanu Valley.

Pages iv/v The Mokulua Islands, known to locals as The Mokes, are two of the several cones, sand bars and rock islands standing off the windward coast of O'ahu.

Page viii Beams of sunlight pierce the cloud cover over Kāne'ohe Bay, lighting a patch of sea and reef.

Page 1 The heart of the visitor experience on O'ahu is Waikīkī, where towering palms vie with highrise hotel, and the calm leeward waters present visitors and residents with a multitude of ocean activities.

Page 1 The moonlight marks a path between the Mokulua Islands at Lanikai, as languid palm fronds droop in the windless evening.

Page 2 The plumeria and orchids, the carnations and 'ilima form a blaze of color at the popular lei stands at Honolulu International Airport.

Page 2 A hula dancer, with a haku lei in her hair, gestures to the sky as the near-vertical Kāne'ohe cliffs rise in the background.

Page 3 The statue of Duke Kahanamoku stands permanently along the shore at Waikīkī, where the Duke once surfed and swam.

Page 4 Running downwind with the light-air sails flying, a racing sloop churns up the sea off Waikīkī.

Page 4 Many bananas are edible, some are used for making rope, and some are just nice to look at, like this ornamental variety, whose pink fruits are packed with seeds.

Page 5 Tuna fishermen haul up their catch off the stern of their boat, often after chumming the water with bait. Note the seabird fishing near the top of the image.

Page 6 The fronds of a palm hang quietly in the sunset on a windless evening.

Page 6 A fragrant yellow ginger lei and a delicate white ginger lei are stretched across many of the other popular flower leis at an island lei stand.

Page 7 Hybridizers have used the common hibiscus to create a wondrous assortment of blossoms in a range of colors, patterns and textures. Here, a frosted pink-red variety.

Pages 8/9 Venerable palms stand by the shore at Kahana Bay. The palm tree, which grows a foot a year, can live for a century or more. They were once grown for the meat in the coconuts, called copra, but in the Islands, they are now mainly used for decorative purposes.

Page 10 A diver swims among the nenue, also known as chub or rudderfish, at Hanauma Bay, an aquatic preserve where fishing is prohibited and marine life is abundant.

Page 10 The beautiful red hibiscus or Chinese rose is closely associated with the Islands, and, although this particular variety is an import, Hawai'i has many species of native hibiscus, some red, some orange, some white and some fragrant.

Page 10 Shoreline fishermen line up their poles at Hālona Point, taking advantage of deep water near the shore to go after the bigger fish, like the powerful ulua or amberjack.

Page 11 The protected crescent of Hanauma Bay, a marine reserve, attracts so many visitors that city officials have been forced to institute limits on its use to control the damage to the ecosystem.

Page 12 Cetaceans leap at Sea Life Park, across the highway from the Makapu'u Beach Park, with the low island Kaohikaipu in the background.

Page 13 Only the most experienced bodysurfers should attack the shorebreak at Sandy Beach when the waves are big. Lifeguards here are kept busy rescuing the inexperienced and unaware, who enter the water in spite of the warnings.

Page 14 Wavelets lit by the moon over Koko Head mark a quiet Hawaiian evening.

Page 14 Surf roaring through the channel between Moloka'i and O'ahu wraps around the eastern end of the island, crashing against the rocks here at Hālona Point.

Page i A windsurfer gets air, driving up off a wave off Diamond Head, a spot where the often-brisk trade winds wrap around the island and create excellent conditions for sailcraft of all kinds.

Page 15 Ships sailing in from the West Coast may pick up the Kalaupapa Light on the north shore of Moloka'i first, but it is the Makapu'u Light, at the eastern tip of O'ahu, that tells them the trip to Honolulu or Pearl Harbor is nearly over.

Page 14 A windsurfer gets air, driving up off a wave off Diamond Head, a spot where the often-brisk trade winds wrap around the island and create excellent conditions for sailcraft of all kinds.

Pages 16/17 Developer Henry Kaiser took the old marshlands of Kuapā Pond and converted them into a waterside development named Hawai'i Kai, now one of the premier bedroom communities on the island.

Pages 18/19 Makapu'u Beach is one of the island's most popular parks for sunning and bodysurfing. The nearshore islands in the background include the flat Kāohikaipu and the tuff cone that forms Mānana or Rabbit Island in the background. It was so named because it once was home to a population of bunnies.

Pages 20/21 Hālona Beach, a quiet patch of sand at the end of a narrow bay, sits at the base of the Hālona Blowhole. The beach is best known, shot from a different angle, as the one where movie stars rolled in the surf in the movie, *From Here to Eternity*.

Pages 22/23 The view through the palms and bougainvillea, seen from Koko Head, is across Maunalua Bay toward Waikīkī.

Page 24 Sandy Beach is one of the most challenging bodysurfing spots in the Islands, and one of the most popular.

Pages 26/27 The sun rises off Diamond Head lighthouse, viewed through the twisted shoreline vegetation.

Page 28 Other surfers dive for protection from a crashing wave as one exhilarated bodysurfer cuts left across the face of a wave at Sandy Beach.

Page 29 A big green sea turtle, a species protected under both federal and state endangered species laws, cruises over. The vegetarian turtles, which eat seaweed, are so named because of the color of their body fat, something fishing families knew well in the days when they were caught for food.

Page 30 Strapped in and ready to go, these windsurfers haven't yet picked up speed, and their boards are still mostly submerged.

Once they are moving well, the boards will skim across the surface, sometimes breaking free to take full flight.

Page 31 An outrigger canoe rigged for sailing cruises toward shore at sunset on Maunalua Bay. If the wind dies, the canoe has a backup outboard motor attached to the stern. If that fails, the crew can always paddle.

Page 32 The sun sets over the ocean on a clear day over Hawai'i, as viewed from the base of Diamond Head, with a classic lighthouse, the venerable Diamond Head Light, outlined in the foreground.

Page 33 The clouds seen from 'Āina Haina are gilded with the light from the setting sun, and framed by coconut palms.

Page 34 Hawaiian aunties and grannies sing and play at the hula show at Kapi'olani Park, one of the classic traditions of Waikīkī.

Page 34 Rental surfboards, seen here on the beach at Waikīkī, take a lot of abuse. Note the gray duct tape patching "dings" in the boards at the back.

Page 35 The waters off Waikīkī are active with boating, most of it originating from the Ala Wai Small Boat Harbor. Sailboat races are held virtually every weekend.

Page 36 A tour catamaran, under power with its sails luffing, cruises the waters off Hawai'i's busiest beach. The stunning weather and calm seas help demonstrate Waikīkī's attraction.

Page 36 An arduous climb up the face of Diamond Head leads to one of the most stunning views in the Islands, with Kapi'olani Park in the foreground, the highrises of Waikīkī, and in the dim distance, the Wai'anae mountain range.

Page 37 A stylized modern version of a Polynesian outrigger takes a sunset cruise off Waikīkī. The craft itself is very different from the wood-and-fiber ones early voyagers used.

Pages 38/39 The classic view of Waikīkī includes Diamond Head, the hotels, the beach full of tourists, and a patch of calm sea. The groins extending into the water were installed to limit the erosion of sand from the beach.

Pages 40/41 At night, Waikīkī lights up. The nearshore waters pick up the reflection of room lights of the upper stories and the dense lighting from the beachfront restaurants and bars.

Page 42 The Pink Palace, the kama'āina's name for the Royal Hawaiian Hotel, was built to house visitors who arrived by steamship. It is situated in a dense garden setting, but is now dwarfed by taller hotels.

Page 43 The waters off Waikīkī are generally calm and protected, but also generally have a small swell that is a favorite for beginning surfers and veteran longboarders who cherish its long tradition of beachboys and hotel nights.

Page 43 A longboard and a tandem ride, one of the regular spectacles on the breaks of Waikīkī.

Page 44 Tourists who have made the long hike up to the summit of Diamond Head pose for a photographer, view the scenery, check out the informative displays, chat and relax before the steep climb back down.

Page 45 If you're a kid with a boogie board, The Wall at Waikīkī is the place to be. It's dense and exhilarating. Even a few adults show up for the ride.

Pages 46/47 Their brightly colored spinnakers leading the way, yachts compete in the regular Friday night races off Waikīkī. The boats generally must beat up from the Ala Wai Small Boat Harbor toward Diamond Head, but catch the wind from astern on the way back.

Pages 48/49 The light of the last bits of sunset paints the white walls of Waikīkī's hotels pink-orange.

Page 50 The red blossom of a bromeliad rises out of the heart of this specimen at Lyon Arboretum in Mānoa Valley.

Page 50 The Mission Houses Museum has some of the oldest extant structures in Waikīkī. The nearer house is built of coral blocks cut locally, while the farther one is of traditional New England frame construction and dates back to 1821.

Page 50 'Iolani Palace, the only royal palace in the nation, was built in 1882 for King Kalākaua. The Hawaiian monarchy last-

ed only another 11 years, until the overthrow of Kalākaua's sister, Queen Lili'uokalani. The palace later served as the territorial capitol, and houses of the state legislature met here during the 1960s.

Page 51 At sunset under the palms, a surfer comes in from the sea at Magic Island, a man-made peninsula between the Ala Wai Small Boat Harbor and Ala Moana Park.

Page 52 The skipper checks the set of his spinnaker while sailing in close quarters during one of the Waikīkī Yacht Club's regular Friday night races off Waikīkī.

Page 52 The rainforest at the top of the Ko'olau Mountains soaks up moisture and releases it gradually, keeping flows like this one over Mānoa Falls running even during the dry season.

Page 53 The Aloha Week court stands for a formal photograph on the steps of 'Iolani Palace, once the home of real Hawaiian royal families. An Aloha Week court is named each year to commemorate Hawai'i's traditions.

Pages 54/55 The inter-island cruise ship USS *Patriot* is tied up at Honolulu Harbor, with Aloha Tower over her bow. The cruise industry is becoming a major part of Hawai'i's visitor industry.

Pages 56/57 A rainbow sets off the Nu'uanu Valley wall. The clouds hanging over the peak of the ridge suggest that the meager waterfalls will soon fill.

Page 58 The War Memorial Natatorium along the sea at Kapi'olani Park, whose decorative entrance opens to reveal a large salt-water swimming pool, has been restored after decades of neglect.

Page 59 The outline of the hull of the battleship USS *Arizona* is visible under the stark white structure of the visitor center built to commemorate its December 7, 1941, sinking in an attack by Japanese warplanes.

Page 59 Boats daily ferry visitors through Pearl Harbor to the USS *Arizona* Memorial. The *Arizona* was one of 18 ships that sank during the attack on the harbor. The disaster opened the U.S. role in World War II in the Pacific.

Page 60 Aloha Tower has long had a commanding view of Honolulu Harbor and much of southern O'ahu. Visitors can ride the elevator to the 10th floor for viewing during the day and early evening.

Page 61 Tantalus or Puʻuʻōhiʻa, on the western arm of Mānoa Valley, is a favored upland home site. Its Hawaiian name refers to the red-flowered metrosideros trees that are one of the species of the Hawaiian forest.

Page 62 The statue of King Kamehameha stands in front of Aliʻiōlani Hale, which now houses the state judiciary. The king's arms and shoulders are draped in flower lei on special occasions.

Page 63 ʻIolani Palace, where Queen Liliʻuokalani was imprisoned after her 1893 overthrow, is now a museum stocked with many of the original items that furnished the palace during the reigns of monarchs Kalākaua and Liliʻuokalani.

Pages 64/65 An aerial view of Honolulu Harbor shows the longline fishing fleet at lower left, a cruise ship at center, and the highrises of downtown Honolulu in the foreground and Waikīkī, in the distance. Diamond Head's familiar profile provides a backdrop.

Page 66 Punchbowl Crater, also known as Pūowaina, is home to the National Memorial Cemetery of the Pacific. The crater is an old tuff cone at the base of the Koʻolau Mountains.

Page 67 Diamond Head is the southernmost promontory on Oʻahu. Here it is seen from at sea, with Kapiʻolani Park's green lawns to the left and developed Honolulu sweeping around its crater.

Pages 68/69 The financial center of Honolulu is readily visible from the dense cluster of high-rises in this photo shot from Pūowaina, or Punchbowl Crater.

Page 70 The developed lands of Honolulu are visible just above the rim of the Koʻolaus in this view from off Waimānalo, where the eroded cliffs rise sharply from the coastline.

Page 71 Aloha Stadium is home to sporting events at the high school, college and professional levels, and also to spectacular entertainment events.

Page 72 The World War II battleship USS *Missouri* is moored along Ford Island in the foreground, with the white USS *Arizona* Memorial structure behind, straddling the sunken hull

of the ship, which was sunk in the December 7, 1941, attack that opened the U.S. role in the war in the Pacific. Strung between the main island and Ford Island is the new vehicular bridge, so Ford Island residents and workers no longer need to depend on boats for access.

Page 72 The massive guns on the USS *Missouri* extend over its wooden decks. Two of the three barrels are fitted with caps to prevent fouling.

Page 73 Canoe paddles of various shapes and uses are leaned against the hull of a fiberglass Malia-mold outrigger canoe. Canoes of this design, among the first fiberglass hulls used in modern outrigger canoeing competition, are taken from the lines of the old koa boat, the *Malia*.

Page 74 Mākua Beach, near the eastern end of the island of Oʻahu, lies at the base of a broad valley used by the Army for training exercises, although the military's use of the valley has been a subject of community opposition.

Page 74 The arid conditions of the southern valleys of the Waiʻanae Mountains limit the amount of sediment that flows into the nearshore waters, keeping the waters clear blue and the sand white, as here at Mākua Beach.

Page 75 Surf higher than 20 feet crashes against the eastern end of Oʻahu at Kaʻena Point. This is the end of the Waiʻanae range, where the military radar and communications facilities line the ridge.

Page 75 Ripples wash silently ashore in the protected waters of Lanikohonua Beach, fronting the Alice Kamokila Campbell estate on Oʻahu's leeward coast.

Page 76 The sun sets over the western horizon as viewed through the palms at Lanikohonua Beach.

Page 76 Viewed from the west, the sparsely vegetated end of the Waiʻanae range displays a reddish dirt color in contrast to the greener areas where the mountains are higher and able to attract more rainfall.

Page 77 Broad Mākua Valley spreads wide between its valley walls as viewed from the calm waters off the western end of Oʻahu.

Page 78 Mākaha Beach is one of the premier surfing spots on the island when the south swell comes up. But, when the ocean is calm, it is a fine spot for family recreation.

Page 80 The man-made beaches at Ko Olina are protected by artificial rock structures and backed by manicured lawns under palms.

Pages 82/83 The palm trees at the Ko Olina resort were planted as adults, brought in from other parts of the Islands, but they readily take the appearance of an old coconut grove.

Page 84 A pretty shorebreak at Mākaha's Papaoneone Beach can be hazardous for beachgoers not familiar with Hawaiʻi coastal conditions.

Page 85 The Waiʻanae Range snakes eastward, with the low Kolekole Pass visible before the lower peak of Puʻu Kalena, and cloud-shrouded Mt. Kaʻala in the distance. Kaʻala is the highest point on the island, at 4,020 feet.

Pages 86/87 Off leeward Oʻahu, the sunsets fill the sky with pastel colors. Here, the day's end is viewed through a grove of coconuts at Ko Olina.

Pages 88/89 The last big beach on the southern Waiʻanae Coast is Keawaʻula Bay, better known to residents as Yokohama Beach.

Page 90 A bodyboarder at the edge of the tube rides the crashing break at Pipeline.

Page 90 Young pineapples with spiked leaves are among the ornamental varieties on display at the Dole Pineapple Pavilion.

Page 90 A net fisherman at Pūpūkea arranges his throw net in preparation for flinging it in a wide circle over schooling fish.

Page 91 A surfer with his yellow "blade" under his right arm strides confidently toward the rolling surf at Waimea Bay.

Page 92 Despite the concern about crowding at Oʻahu surf sites, most of the waves that come ashore are never ridden, including this shorebreak with a nice tube at Waimea Bay.

Page 92 A carved tiki held around the neck with a bungee cord decorates the entrance to a Haleʻiwa surf shop. In the background, an old wood frame building demonstrates some of the historic architecture of this picturesque North Shore community.

Page 93 Dillingham Airfield, between Mokulē'ia Beach and the Wai'anae Mountains, is a favorite takeoff point for glider pilots. On the sand, the tracks of numerous vehicles are visible. While beach driving is a common practice, it is extremely destructive to native species that use the beach, like sea turtle nests and sand crab burrows.

Page 94 Surfers check out the scene at Sunset Beach, but there's not much surf to be seen.

Page 95 The crescent of sand at Waimea Bay in calm weather is picturesque. Daring youngsters often leap from the nearshore rock island. But in winter swells, the region is a raging mass of whitewater.

Pages 96/97 Footprints below the high water mark at Mokulē'ia Beach lead out toward the end of the Wai'anae Mountains and Ka'ena Point, the eastern end of O'ahu.

Page 98 A lifeguard keeps track of the beachgoers in this late afternoon scene at Sunset Beach.

Page 99 The golf course in early morning at Kuilima, often referred to as Turtle Cove.

Pages 100/101 The setting sun turns the sky pink and paints the waters of Kawela Bay on O'ahu's North Shore.

Page 102 Surf rolls onto the shore at Pūpūkea Beach Park, breaking on the rocky shelves.

Page 104/105 Kukaniloko State Monument in Wahiawā, viewed here at sunset, is one of the most sacred places on the island of O'ahu. It is a place where the mothers of children destined to be chiefs were brought to give birth.

Pages 106/107 The sands of Banzai Beach near Sunset Beach are empty in the early morning.

Page 108 Mokulē'ia Beach heads eastward in this aerial shot to the twin bays of Kaiaka and Waialua, where the coastline turns north toward Kahuku Point.

Page 109 There is nothing quite so refreshing as a chilly shave ice treat on the bench fronting Matsumoto Shave Ice in Hale'iwa.

Pages 110/111 From Waimea Bay, the sun sets off the end of the island, beyond Ka'ena Point.

Page 112 A bodyboarder is about to take the plunge in big surf at Waimea Bay.

Page 113 The Eddie Aikau surf meet is held only when the waves are big enough, as here, where experienced longboarders prepare to ride some of the biggest waves that roll into Hawai'i shores.

Page 114 A surfer races down the face as the lip begins to curl over his head. When it cuts loose, tons of water will crash down on the lower part of the wave.

Page 115 A board surfer gets tubed at Pipeline. He will ride for as long as possible inside a culvert made of water.

Page 116 Petroglyphs or rock drawings, shown here in this late Windward O'ahu, often include images of human figures. Sexual identifiers are uncommon, but here one image is clearly male and one may be viewed as giving birth.

Page 116 A modern outrigger sailing canoe is prepared for an outing at Kailua Beach. One steering paddle is tucked behind the steersman's seat, and a spare leans against the canoe's hull.

Page 117 The tranquil waters at Ka'a'awa Beach are protected from the surf by an offshore reef, its location identifiable in the distance by the white line of the waves.

Page 118 A couple walks the beach, another sits and talks, and a solitary sunbather catches rays at Kailua Beach.

Page 118 The jagged peak of Olomana pierces the landscape mauka of Kailua. An arduous hike along a rugged trail leads one to its summit.

Page 119 The Hawaiian voyaging canoe Hokule'a eases into Kāne'ohe Bay with Mokoli'i Island in the background.

Page 119 The distinctive shape of Mokoli'i Island, also known as Chinaman's Hat, stands out against the sunrise, viewed from Kualoa Beach Park.

Page 120 The dredged channels leading into and around Coconut Island are readily visible from above. The island, once a getaway for wealthy owners, is now primarily used for marine research.

Page 120 A pair of outrigger sailing canoes lie at anchor at the western end of Kāne'ohe Bay, with Mokoli'i Island, commonly called Chinaman's Hat, in the background.

Page 121 A humpback whale breaches off Kāne'ohe. The whales appear in the islands each fall and remain through the spring, when they head back into colder waters off Alaska.

Pages 122/123 The peak of Pu'ukānehoalani rises above steep cliffs, with Mokoli'i Island visible off the shore to the right. Viewed from Waiāhole Beach Park.

Pages 124/125 The twin islands known as the Mokes, or Mokulua Islands, as seen from the ridge behind the community known as Lanikai. Mokulua simply means two islands.

Pages 126/127 Ho'omaluhia Park is a botanical garden at the base of the Kāne'ohe cliffs, operated by the City and County of Honolulu.

Page 128 A recreational sailing boat is hauled up on the small beach of one of the Mokulua Islands.

Page 129 Shallow, sand-dominated nearshore waters at Waimānalo Beach are safe for swimming and favored for recreational use by light sailing craft.

Page 130 Little evidence of O'ahu's urban nature is visible in the mountainous heart of the island, as here in the Ko'olau Mountains.

Page 131 A sailboarder throws up a big wake while speeding toward shore in Kāne'ohe Bay.

Page 136 The rising moon lights a pale highway across the ocean between the Mokulua Islands.

MOONRISE OVER THE MOKULUA ISLANDS, LANIKAI